EMMANUEL JOSEPH

The UK's Dual Role, Balancing Military Power and International Aid

Copyright © 2025 by Emmanuel Joseph

All rights reserved. No part of this publication may be reproduced, stored or transmitted in any form or by any means, electronic, mechanical, photocopying, recording, scanning, or otherwise without written permission from the publisher. It is illegal to copy this book, post it to a website, or distribute it by any other means without permission.

First edition

This book was professionally typeset on Reedsy.
Find out more at reedsy.com

Contents

1	Chapter 1	1
2	Chapter 1: The Historical Evolution of British Military...	3
3	Chapter 2: The Rise of International Aid Programs	5
4	Chapter 3: The Integration of Military and Aid Efforts	7
5	Chapter 4: Case Study: Afghanistan	9
6	Chapter 5: Challenges in Balancing Military and Aid	11
7	Chapter 6: Ethical Considerations in Military and Aid...	13
8	Chapter 7: The Role of Technology in Enhancing Military and...	15
9	Chapter 8: Partnerships and Collaborations	17
10	Chapter 9: Domestic Perspectives and Public Opinion	19
11	Chapter 10: Future Challenges and Emerging Threats	21
12	Chapter 11: Lessons Learned from Past Missions	23
13	Chapter 12: Conclusion: The Path Forward	25

1

Chapter 1

Introduction

In a rapidly evolving global landscape, the United Kingdom's ability to balance military power with international aid represents a unique and complex aspect of its foreign policy. This dual role underscores the nation's commitment to safeguarding global security while simultaneously addressing humanitarian needs across the world. The UK's historical evolution, marked by its colonial past and subsequent transformation into a modern state, has shaped its current approach to wielding both military influence and humanitarian support.

As conflicts, natural disasters, and crises continue to challenge nations, the UK's integrated strategy of leveraging military capabilities to support humanitarian missions has become increasingly vital. This multifaceted approach allows the UK to respond to immediate threats and emergencies while fostering long-term stability and development in affected regions. The importance of this balance cannot be overstated, as it reflects the UK's dedication to upholding human rights, promoting peace, and contributing to global prosperity.

Through this book, we will explore the historical context, strategic developments, and ethical considerations that define the UK's dual role. By examining case studies, partnerships, and future challenges, we aim to provide a comprehensive understanding of how the UK navigates the intricate interplay between military power and international aid. This exploration will highlight the successes, lessons learned, and ongoing efforts to refine and enhance this delicate balance.

The UK's dual role is not without its challenges, but it remains a testament to the nation's resilience, adaptability, and unwavering commitment to global well-being. As we delve into each chapter, we invite readers to consider the broader implications of balancing military might with humanitarian compassion, and how this approach can serve as a model for other nations striving to address the complex demands of our interconnected world.

2

Chapter 1: The Historical Evolution of British Military Power

The UK's military power has deep historical roots that trace back to the times of the British Empire. Over centuries, the British military evolved from a collection of regional forces to a unified and formidable global presence. The conquests and colonies established by the British Empire were both defended and expanded through the use of military might. This era showcased the strategic importance of a strong military in asserting and maintaining national dominance.

Post-World War II, the nature of military power began to shift. The UK's role in the world changed as it transitioned from an empire to a key player in global security alliances like NATO. The focus moved from outright conquest to maintaining peace and stability in various regions. Despite the reduction in the number of colonies, the UK's military continued to play a significant role in international conflict resolution and peacekeeping efforts.

In modern times, the UK's military power is characterized by its advanced technological capabilities and highly trained personnel. The development of nuclear capabilities, sophisticated defense systems, and cutting-edge intelligence services are indicative of this transformation. The UK's military strategy now encompasses a range of activities from counter-terrorism to cyber warfare, reflecting the complexities of contemporary global threats.

Additionally, the UK's defense policy is shaped by its commitment to international partnerships. By collaborating with allies and contributing to global military initiatives, the UK reinforces its position as a leader in maintaining international security. This chapter provides a comprehensive look at how the UK's military power has evolved over the years, adapting to new challenges and continuously striving to uphold global stability.

3

Chapter 2: The Rise of International Aid Programs

Parallel to its military developments, the UK has also established itself as a leader in international aid. The roots of these efforts can be found in the aftermath of World War II, when the UK played a pivotal role in the reconstruction of Europe through initiatives like the Marshall Plan. This period marked the beginning of the UK's enduring commitment to providing humanitarian assistance to nations in need.

The establishment of the Department for International Development (DFID) in 1997 marked a significant milestone in the UK's aid efforts. DFID was tasked with coordinating and managing the UK's international aid programs, focusing on poverty alleviation, health, education, and sustainable development. Under its guidance, the UK's aid contributions have grown, positioning the country as one of the leading donors in the world.

The UK's aid programs are characterized by their strategic focus and long-term vision. Rather than simply providing immediate relief, these programs aim to address the root causes of poverty and instability. By investing in infrastructure, education, and healthcare, the UK helps to build the foundations for sustainable development in recipient countries. This holistic approach ensures that aid efforts have a lasting impact.

Furthermore, the UK's aid strategy emphasizes partnerships with international organizations, non-governmental organizations (NGOs), and recipient governments. This collaborative approach enhances the effectiveness of aid programs by leveraging the expertise and resources of various stakeholders. Through these partnerships, the UK ensures that its aid efforts are well-coordinated and aligned with the needs and priorities of the communities it serves.

4

Chapter 3: The Integration of Military and Aid Efforts

One of the defining features of the UK's foreign policy is its ability to integrate military and aid efforts. This dual approach allows the UK to address both the immediate and long-term needs of conflict-affected regions. By deploying military resources in support of humanitarian missions, the UK maximizes the impact of its efforts.

In conflict zones, the UK military often plays a crucial role in providing security and stability, creating a safe environment for aid delivery. This involves tasks such as clearing mines, protecting aid convoys, and establishing secure zones for displaced populations. The presence of military forces can deter violence and facilitate the safe distribution of humanitarian assistance.

Conversely, the UK's aid programs contribute to the long-term stability of conflict-affected regions by addressing the underlying causes of instability. Initiatives focused on education, economic development, and governance help to build resilient communities capable of sustaining peace. By fostering development, the UK reduces the likelihood of future conflicts and enhances the prospects for lasting peace.

The integration of military and aid efforts is exemplified by the UK's involvement in multi-dimensional peacekeeping missions. In these missions, military personnel work alongside humanitarian workers to provide comprehensive support to affected populations. This collaborative approach ensures that both immediate needs and long-term development goals are addressed, demonstrating the UK's commitment to a balanced and effective foreign policy.

5

Chapter 4: Case Study: Afghanistan

Afghanistan serves as a critical case study in understanding the UK's dual role of balancing military power and international aid. The UK's involvement in Afghanistan began in 2001, as part of the NATO-led coalition to combat terrorism and stabilize the region. Over the years, the UK's military efforts have been complemented by significant aid contributions aimed at rebuilding the war-torn country.

On the military front, the UK's objectives included dismantling terrorist networks, supporting Afghan security forces, and restoring order. These efforts were instrumental in weakening the Taliban's control and creating a more secure environment for Afghan citizens. The presence of UK troops also facilitated the delivery of humanitarian aid and the implementation of development projects.

The aid programs in Afghanistan focused on a wide range of areas, including education, healthcare, infrastructure, and governance. The UK invested heavily in building schools, hospitals, and roads, as well as supporting democratic institutions. These efforts aimed to improve the quality of life for Afghans and lay the groundwork for sustainable development.

Despite the challenges and complexities of the mission, the UK's dual approach in Afghanistan underscores the importance of balancing military power with international aid. The lessons learned from this experience highlight the need for a coordinated and comprehensive strategy that addresses both security and development. By integrating military and aid efforts, the UK has made significant contributions to Afghanistan's progress, while also acknowledging the ongoing challenges that remain.

6

Chapter 5: Challenges in Balancing Military and Aid

Balancing military power and international aid presents a range of challenges for the UK. One of the primary challenges is ensuring that both efforts are adequately funded and resourced. Military operations and aid programs often compete for limited budgetary allocations, requiring careful prioritization and strategic planning.

Another challenge is the potential for conflicting objectives between military and aid missions. Military operations are typically focused on achieving security and stability, while aid programs aim to address humanitarian and development needs. Reconciling these differing priorities requires effective coordination and communication between military and aid agencies.

The dynamic and complex nature of modern conflicts further complicates the balancing act. Humanitarian crises often arise in conflict zones, necessitating the simultaneous deployment of military and aid resources. Navigating these challenging environments requires adaptability and flexibility in both military and aid strategies.

Additionally, the UK's dual role is subject to scrutiny from both domestic and international audiences. Public opinion and political pressures can influence the allocation of resources and the prioritization of missions. Ensuring transparency and accountability in both military and aid efforts is essential to maintaining public trust and support for the UK's foreign policy.

7

Chapter 6: Ethical Considerations in Military and Aid Efforts

The UK's dual role in balancing military power and international aid is guided by a strong ethical framework. This framework emphasizes the importance of protecting human rights, upholding international law, and promoting the welfare of vulnerable populations. Ethical considerations play a crucial role in shaping the UK's approach to both military and aid missions.

In military operations, the UK is committed to minimizing harm to civilians and adhering to the principles of proportionality and necessity. This involves implementing strict rules of engagement, conducting thorough risk assessments, and prioritizing the protection of civilian lives. By adhering to these principles, the UK aims to ensure that its military actions are just and responsible.

Similarly, ethical considerations underpin the UK's aid programs. The UK prioritizes the needs and rights of the most vulnerable populations, ensuring that aid is distributed fairly and equitably. The principles of impartiality, neutrality, and independence guide the delivery of humanitarian assistance, ensuring that aid reaches those who need it most, regardless of political or military affiliations.

The UK's commitment to ethical conduct is reinforced by its engagement with international organizations and adherence to global standards. By collaborating with partners such as the United Nations and the Red Cross, the UK ensures that its military and aid efforts align with internationally recognized principles and best practices. This ethical approach enhances the credibility and legitimacy of the UK's dual role on the global stage.

8

Chapter 7: The Role of Technology in Enhancing Military and Aid Efforts

Advancements in technology have significantly enhanced the UK's ability to balance military power and international aid. In the military sphere, cutting-edge technologies such as drones, artificial intelligence, and cybersecurity capabilities have revolutionized the way the UK conducts operations. These technologies enable more precise and efficient military actions, reducing the risk of collateral damage and enhancing the effectiveness of missions.

Similarly, technology plays a vital role in the delivery of international aid. Innovations such as mobile health applications, remote sensing, and blockchain technology have improved the efficiency and transparency of aid programs. These technologies enable real-time monitoring of aid distribution, enhance data collection and analysis, and facilitate secure and transparent financial transactions.

The integration of technology in both military and aid efforts also fosters greater collaboration and coordination. For example, satellite imagery and geospatial data can be used to assess the impact of conflicts and disasters, informing both military and aid responses. Communication technologies enable seamless coordination between military personnel and humanitarian workers, ensuring that efforts are well-coordinated and complementary.

However, the reliance on technology also presents new challenges and ethical considerations. The use of autonomous weapons and surveillance technologies raises questions about accountability and the protection of human rights. Ensuring that technological advancements are used responsibly and ethically is essential to maintaining the integrity of the UK's dual role.

9

Chapter 8: Partnerships and Collaborations

The UK's ability to balance military power and international aid is strengthened by its partnerships and collaborations with other nations and international organizations. These partnerships enhance the UK's capacity to address global challenges and ensure that its efforts are well-coordinated and impactful.

In the military realm, the UK is an active member of international alliances such as NATO. These alliances facilitate joint military exercises, information sharing, and coordinated responses to global threats. By working with other nations, the UK enhances its military capabilities and contributes to collective security.

International aid efforts are also bolstered by partnerships with organizations like the United Nations, the World Bank, and various non-governmental organizations (NGOs). These collaborations enable the UK to pool resources, share expertise, and implement large-scale aid programs. Through multilateral initiatives, the UK can address complex humanitarian challenges that no single nation could tackle alone.

Partnerships also extend to regional organizations and bilateral relationships. The UK works closely with the European Union, the African Union, and other regional bodies to address specific regional issues. Bilateral partnerships with countries like the United States, Canada, and Japan further strengthen the UK's ability to deliver both military and aid missions effectively.

The success of these partnerships relies on effective communication, mutual trust, and shared goals. The UK's commitment to transparency and accountability in its military and aid efforts fosters strong relationships with its partners. By continuing to build and nurture these partnerships, the UK can amplify its impact and contribute to global peace and development.

10

Chapter 9: Domestic Perspectives and Public Opinion

The UK's dual role in balancing military power and international aid is shaped by domestic perspectives and public opinion. Within the UK, there are diverse views on the allocation of resources between military and aid efforts. Political parties, policymakers, and the general public often engage in debates on the priorities and objectives of the UK's foreign policy.

Public opinion plays a significant role in influencing government decisions on military and aid spending. Events such as military interventions or humanitarian crises can sway public sentiment and shape the national discourse. The government's ability to effectively communicate the rationale and outcomes of its military and aid efforts is crucial in garnering public support.

Political parties and policymakers have varying views on the balance between military power and international aid. Some advocate for a stronger focus on defense and security, while others emphasize the importance of humanitarian assistance and development. These differing perspectives reflect broader debates on the UK's role in the world and its responsibilities as a global actor.

The media also plays a key role in shaping public opinion on military and aid issues. Media coverage of conflicts, humanitarian crises, and government policies can influence public perceptions and generate discussions on the UK's foreign policy. Understanding and addressing domestic perspectives is essential for the UK to effectively balance its dual role and maintain public support for its international engagements.

11

Chapter 10: Future Challenges and Emerging Threats

Looking ahead, the UK faces a range of future challenges and emerging threats that will impact its ability to balance military power and international aid. Climate change, global pandemics, and technological advancements are among the key issues that require innovative and adaptive strategies.

Climate change poses significant risks to global stability and human security. The increasing frequency and severity of natural disasters, such as hurricanes, floods, and droughts, necessitate a coordinated response from both military and aid agencies. The UK's ability to address these challenges will require a comprehensive approach that integrates disaster preparedness, resilience building, and sustainable development.

Global pandemics, as demonstrated by the COVID-19 crisis, highlight the interconnectedness of global health and security. The UK's response to future pandemics will require a combination of military logistics, medical expertise, and international aid. Strengthening global health systems and ensuring equitable access to vaccines and treatments will be crucial in mitigating the impact of future health crises.

Technological advancements, including cyber warfare and artificial intelligence, present both opportunities and challenges for the UK's dual role. The development and deployment of advanced technologies can enhance military capabilities and improve the delivery of aid. However, these technologies also introduce new risks and ethical considerations that must be carefully managed.

By proactively addressing these future challenges and emerging threats, the UK can continue to effectively balance its military power and international aid efforts. This requires a forward-thinking approach, international collaboration, and a commitment to innovation and resilience.

12

Chapter 11: Lessons Learned from Past Missions

Reflecting on past missions, the UK has gained valuable lessons in balancing military power and international aid. Case studies from various conflicts and humanitarian interventions provide insights into the successes, challenges, and areas for improvement in the UK's approach.

One key lesson is the importance of strategic planning and coordination. Successful missions have demonstrated the need for comprehensive planning that integrates military and aid objectives. Effective coordination between military personnel, humanitarian workers, and local partners is essential in achieving mission goals and maximizing impact.

Another lesson is the significance of cultural sensitivity and community engagement. Understanding the cultural, social, and political context of the regions in which the UK operates is crucial for the success of both military and aid efforts. Engaging with local communities, respecting their traditions, and involving them in decision-making processes enhances the effectiveness and sustainability of interventions.

The importance of adaptability and flexibility is also highlighted in past missions. Conflicts and humanitarian crises are dynamic and unpredictable, requiring the UK to adapt its strategies and respond to changing circumstances. This involves being prepared for contingencies, learning from experiences, and continuously improving operational approaches.

By drawing on these lessons and applying them to future missions, the UK can refine its dual approach to military power and international aid. Continuous learning and improvement ensure that the UK remains a responsive and effective global actor.

13

Chapter 12: Conclusion: The Path Forward

In conclusion, the UK's dual role in balancing military power and international aid is a defining feature of its foreign policy. The historical evolution of the UK's military and aid efforts, the integration of these approaches, and the lessons learned from past missions underscore the importance of a balanced and strategic approach.

As the UK faces future challenges and emerging threats, it must continue to innovate and adapt. This requires a commitment to ethical conduct, international collaboration, and the effective use of technology. By maintaining a balanced approach, the UK can address both security threats and humanitarian needs, contributing to global peace and development.

The UK's ability to navigate the complexities of military power and international aid will be crucial in shaping its role on the world stage. By fostering partnerships, engaging with domestic perspectives, and drawing on lessons from the past, the UK can continue to make a meaningful impact in addressing global challenges.

Ultimately, the UK's dual role reflects its commitment to promoting stability, human rights, and development worldwide. By balancing military power with international aid, the UK sets an example for other nations and demonstrates the importance of a comprehensive and compassionate approach to global engagement.

Book Description

In "The UK's Dual Role: Balancing Military Power and International Aid," we embark on a compelling journey through the intricate dynamics that define the United Kingdom's foreign policy. This book delves into the historical evolution, strategic developments, and ethical considerations that shape the UK's unique approach to wielding military power while extending a helping hand through international aid.

Through twelve well-crafted chapters, readers will gain an in-depth understanding of how the UK navigates the delicate balance between addressing immediate security threats and fostering long-term stability in conflict-affected regions. From examining historical contexts and modern military strategies to exploring the pivotal role of international aid programs and partnerships, this book provides a comprehensive overview of the UK's dual role on the global stage.

Case studies, such as the UK's involvement in Afghanistan, offer valuable insights into the successes and challenges of integrating military and humanitarian efforts. The book also highlights the importance of ethical conduct, technological advancements, and the influence of domestic perspectives in shaping the UK's foreign policy.

As we face an increasingly complex and interconnected world, "The UK's Dual Role" serves as a timely and thought-provoking exploration of how one nation strives to uphold global security and promote human rights. This book not only sheds light on the UK's past and present efforts but also offers a forward-looking perspective on the future challenges and opportunities in balancing military power with international aid. Through meticulous research and insightful analysis, this book aims to inspire a deeper understanding of the UK's commitment to global peace and development.

www.ingramcontent.com/pod-product-compliance
Lightning Source LLC
LaVergne TN
LVHW020742090526
838202LV00057BA/6192